How to draw and paint
PEOPLE

Contents

Getting started

Anyone can paint and draw people – it is just a matter of developing the talent. It is like learning to play football, or tennis, or a musical instrument – practice every day and you will find you get better and better. This book will give you lots of ideas to try out at home or at school.

There are all sorts of different paints, papers and drawing materials in the shops. It is important to choose the right materials for each kind of artwork. They are described in later chapters – but here are some items you will need when you start painting and drawing.

Brushes

It is important to have good paint brushes. The ones that come in most painting sets aren't very good – they are too floppy and the hairs fall out. Ask for brushes made of hog's hair or nylon. They are not too expensive, and they last a long time. You will need a small watercolor brush that comes to a point, for painting small details, and a large brush with a longer handle for painting big shapes.

Paper

There are several kinds of paper, and it comes in a variety of colors. You can buy paper in sheets or in pads. *Newsprint* is fine if you are using powder paints, pastels or crayons. An *all-purpose paper* has a nice surface for pencil drawing. You can buy special paper for painting in watercolor. Because it is white, it makes your paint colors really sparkle. It is also a good idea to buy a small sketch pad which you can carry around with you.

Paint palettes

You can buy special paint palettes for mixing your paints, but old dishes and plates do just as well – the bigger the better, so you have plenty of room to mix your colors.

Drawing board

You will need a hard surface to support your paper when you draw and paint. You can buy one ready-made, or make one from blockboard or plywood. Use clips or thumbtacks to attach the paper to the board.

Tips

So you've bought your paint, papers and brushes and you're ready to paint a masterpiece! Here are some tips to help you get started.

- **Keep it clean** Wear old clothes when you are painting, or borrow an old shirt to protect your clothes from paint splashes.

- **Get organized** Make sure you have everything you need *before* you start.

- **Prevent accidents** Give yourself lots of room; it will stop you spilling water jars or knocking things onto the floor. If you are right-handed keep your paints and water jar on your right side, or the other way round if you are left-handed. This stops you dripping paint on your paper when you reach over to dip your brush.

- **Save it** Save money, and help protect the environment by re-using materials that normally get thrown away. For instance, save old jars, dinner plates and plastic pots for mixing paints. (Liquid detergent bottles with the tops cut off are useful too.) Cut up old clothes to make rags for mopping up. Collect newspapers for protecting your work table (and the floor!) Save small objects like bottle tops, buttons, dried pasta shapes and shiny candy wrappers for when you make collage pictures. Use scrap paper for testing pencils, brushes and paint mixes.

Drawing heads

B efore you learn how to draw the different features of the face – the eyes, ears, nose and mouth – you first need to know how to draw heads, and how to find the correct position to place the features on the face. It is difficult to know where to begin. Sometimes we make the nose too long, or place the eyes too high up on the face. Sometimes we put the mouth too low, or the ears in the wrong place. Here are some tips that will help you avoid making mistakes.

How the head sits on the neck
When you draw a figure, be careful not to draw the neck too thin.
The drawing on the right is correct.
The neck is nearly as wide as the face (check this for yourself by looking in the mirror!)

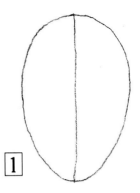

Arty says…
Cut out faces and heads from magazines and newspapers and trace over them. It's a good way to learn where the features are positioned.

How to draw a head
Seen from the front, the head is shaped like an egg, with the pointed end down.

Start by drawing the shape of the head. Then draw a line down the middle of the head. This gives you the position for the nose and the centre of the mouth.

The hairline is about one-third down from the top of the head to the eyes.

Draw a line across the middle of the head. This is where the eyes are positioned.

The eyes are halfway down the head.

The ears line up between the eyebrows and the tip of the nose.

Draw another line halfway below that. This is where the tip of the nose will come. Draw another line halfway between the nose line and the bottom of the chin. This is where the mouth will go. Now you can draw in the eyes, nose and mouth in their correct positions. The ears line up between the eyebrows and the tip of the nose.

The tip of the nose is halfway between the eyebrows and the bottom of the chin.

The lower lip is halfway between the tip of the nose and the bottom of the chin.

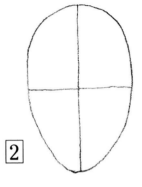
1

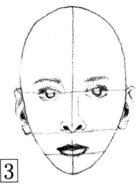
2

3

Egg-heads

We don't always see people's faces from straight in front. When someone is looking up, down, or to one side, their head is tilted at an angle – and this makes the features even more difficult to draw! You can make a simple model that will help you to see what happens to the features of the face when the head is tilted at different angles.

Take a hard-boiled egg and hold it pointed end down. Using the measuring method above, draw eyes and a mouth on the egg. Make a nose out of plasticine and stick it on the egg. Tip the "egg-head" forwards, backwards and to either side.

Make drawings of your egg-head model from different angles.

5

Eyes

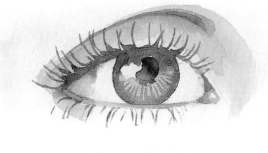

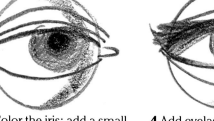

When we look at a person, we usually notice their eyes first. The eyes are the most expressive feature of the face – they can tell us a lot about a person's feelings.

Eyes differ in shape, size and color from one person to another. But everyone's eyes are made in the same way. You will find it easier to draw and paint eyes if you understand how they are formed. Let's take a closer look at eyes.

Below: It helps to understand how eyes fit into the skull in order to draw them. You only see part of an eyeball – the rest is hidden behind the eyelids. Use your fingertip gently to feel the roundness of your eyeballs through your upper eyelids.

With what you know about eye shapes, you can start drawing them in step-by-step stages.

Right: Eye shapes vary a lot. Look how the upper and lower eyelids curve on each eye – for example, the bottom lid on the top eye is almost flat, but its top lid is much more curved. The middle eye's curves are almost identical. Look at the eye corners – in the top and bottom eyes, they are level with each other, but on the middle eye they are on a slope.

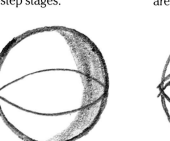  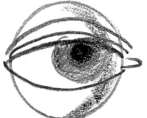 

1 To draw an eye from the front, draw a circle for the eyeball. Add eyelids, with the corners on the ball sides.

2 Outline the pupil, and add a line to show the eyelid thickness. Shade the dark side of the eyeball.

3 Color the iris; add a small loop on the right corner for the tear duct. A rough line shows the eyebrow.

4 Add eyelashes to complete the eye. Highlights on the iris and pupil will make the eye look really round and shiny.

1 The opening of an eye seen from the side looks like a slice of cake, with its corner in the eyeball center.

2 Add shading to one side of your eyeball to give it real shape and a feeling of solidity.

3 When you draw the iris and the pupil, you will not be able to see all of them – they should be oval shaped.

4 Finish the eye with some eyelashes – don't forget that upper eyelashes are longer than lower ones.

The distance between eyes varies slightly from person to person. Usually, however, you'll find the distance between the two inner eye corners is about one eye width, as shown right.

Your eyes are a dead giveaway when it comes to showing your emotions! Without looking at the captions to the pairs of eyes below, see if you can tell what sort of emotion each pair of eyes is showing.

This person's eyes have been crying – the edges of the eyelids are red, and there are shiny highlights on the lower eyelids.

This pair of eyes suggest someone smiling. The eyes look straight forward and there are wrinkles – "laughter lines" – around the eye.

This person looks worried and thoughtful – perhaps he's wondering how he did in an exam!

If you are scared of spiders, this is how you'd look if you saw one on your wrist!

You can't believe what you're hearing, and your eyes are wide open in astonishment!

People who are angry squeeze their eyelids together – the closer they are, the angrier the expression.

Mouths

The mouth is a very expressive part of the face. A smiling mouth tells us that someone is happy, but lips that are tight and thin tell us that someone is angry. When you paint or draw a portrait, pay special attention to the mouth, because its shape and expression are part of the character of the face. Here are some useful tips to help you to draw and paint mouths realistically.

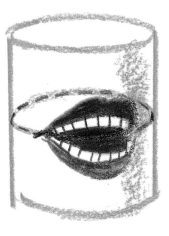

The lips are not flat and straight, but follow the curve of the teeth. Imagine the face as a cylinder – like a can of peas!

When the face is turned a little to one side, you can see the curved shape of the mouth more clearly.

When a person laughs, you can see clearly how the lips are drawn back over the curve of the teeth.

You can show the curved shape of the lips in your paintings and drawings by using the contrast of light and shade. This mouth looks flat because it has been painted all one color.

This mouth looks more realistic because the artist used a darker shade for the shadowed parts of the lips and a lighter shade for the parts that stick out and catch the light.

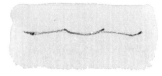

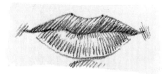

How to draw the mouth
1 Start by drawing the dark line between the lips.

2 Very lightly draw the outline of the upper and lower lips.

3 Look carefully for the patches of light and shadow on the lips. Start by shading in the lightest parts, using very light pencil strokes.

4 Add more pencil strokes to shade in the dark areas. Don't forget the tiny shadow underneath the bottom lip.

The mouth from the front

Notice how some parts of the lips look paler than others, where the light hits them.

The top lip is usually thinner and a little longer than the bottom lip. There are small shadows at the corners.

The line between the lips is the darkest part. Often there is a shadow just underneath this line.

There is a small shadow under the bottom lip.

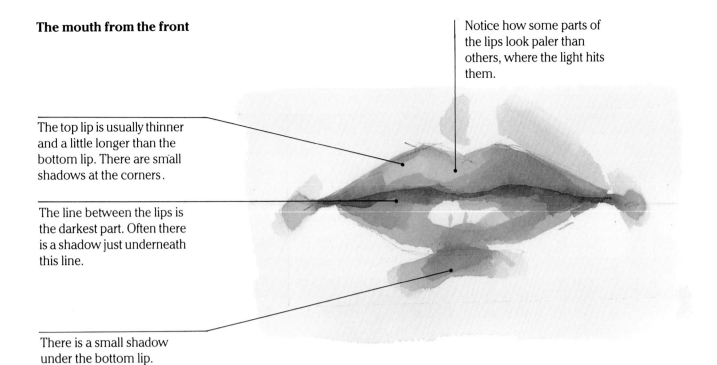

The mouth from the side

The top lip sticks out slightly further than the bottom lip.

The top lip is thinner than the bottom lip.

The bottom lip is paler because it catches more light.

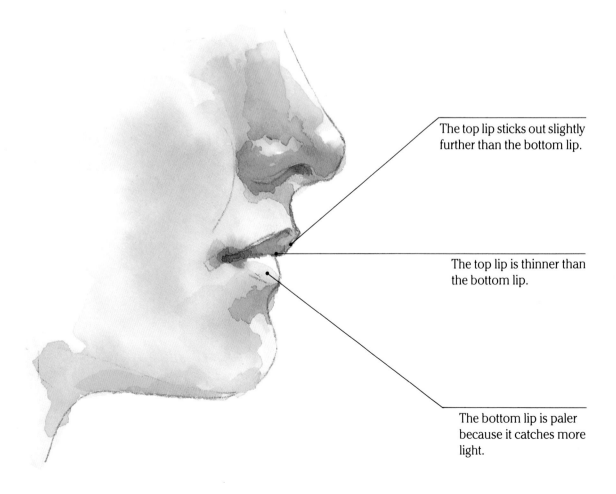

Noses and ears

When you draw noses, look carefully at the areas of light and shadow that reveal their form. Leave the light parts white and shade in the shadowed parts. This is how artists show the way the nose sticks out from the face – without light and shadow, the nose would look flat.

Drawing a nose from the front

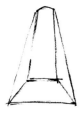

1 The middle section is a wedge shape.

2 The tip is ball-shaped.

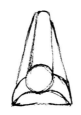

3 The nostrils are wing-shaped.

Drawing a nose from the side

1 The basic shape is a triangle.

2 The tip is ball-shaped.

3 The nostril is wing-shaped.

There is usually a dark shadow beneath the nose, and another shadow down one side. The bridge of the nose (the bony part down the middle) catches the light, and so does the soft tip of the nose. The nostrils are the darkest parts.

When you have the shape right, rub out the guide lines or draw on top of them and fill in the areas of light and shadow with pencil strokes.

Look at people in a line at the supermarket checkout. You'll see an amazing variety of ears and noses!

Ears

You can draw friends' ears while they watch television or chat. Draw the ears from the front (some people's ears stick out more than others!) Then move around to one side of your model and draw the ear from full view. This is more difficult, because the ear is such a funny shape. When you look into the ear you can see the strange, uncurling forms, as if it was searching for sound. Don't worry if your first drawings are not very good. Keep practicing and you will get better and better!

This drawing shows the position of the ear on the side of the head. It lines up with the eyebrow at the top and the tip of the nose at the bottom. Its position is in the middle of the head – farther away from the face than you might think.

Drawing an ear

1 Draw the outline of the ear first.

2 Draw the earhole.

3 Fit the spiralling shapes in between.

4 Look for the shadows inside the ear and shade them in.

From the front, the ear is a squashed-up shape. Look for the contrast between light and shadow.

11

Measuring the body

When you draw or paint a picture of someone, do you sometimes find that you have made the head too big, or the legs too short, or the hands too small? If you want your pictures of people to look realistic, you have to get all the different parts of the body in correct *proportion*. At first you may think this is very hard – no two bodies are exactly the same. What's more, the younger someone is, the bigger the head is in relation to the rest of the body. Luckily, whether a person is young or old, short or tall, or fat or thin, there are some simple rules to help you get different parts of the body looking right and in proportion to each other.

In babies, the head goes about 4 times into the height of the body.

In older children, the head goes about 6 times into the height of the body.

When the arms are stretched out, the length from the fingertips of one hand to the fingertips of the other hand is equal to the height of the body.

Adult proportions

In adults, the head goes about 7 times into the height of the body.

The elbow comes about halfway down the arm.

The legs start about halfway down the body.

When the arms hang at the sides, the tips of the fingers reach down to halfway between the hips and the knees.

The knees are about halfway down the legs.

Drawing the body

The human body is made up of many complicated shapes, so it is easier to draw if you start with soft pencil guidelines, breaking it down into simple shapes first. Think of the body as being made up of little scraps – rather like the Tin Man from the film *The Wizard of* *Oz*. The head is shaped like an egg, the arms and legs like sausages, and so on. Following the steps below, you can make your own "Tin Man." When you have completed your "Tin Man" drawing, you can start to build up the different parts of the body in more detail to make your picture more realistic.

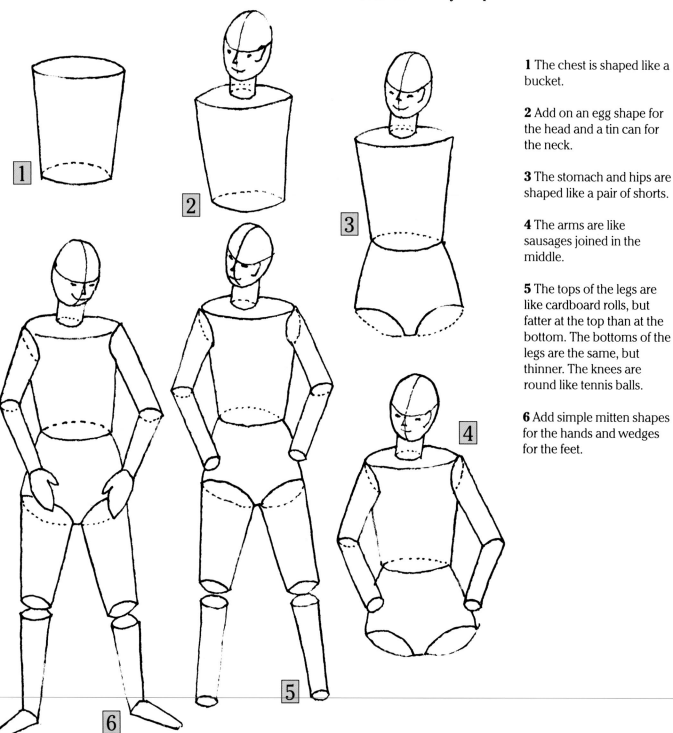

1 The chest is shaped like a bucket.

2 Add on an egg shape for the head and a tin can for the neck.

3 The stomach and hips are shaped like a pair of shorts.

4 The arms are like sausages joined in the middle.

5 The tops of the legs are like cardboard rolls, but fatter at the top than at the bottom. The bottoms of the legs are the same, but thinner. The knees are round like tennis balls.

6 Add simple mitten shapes for the hands and wedges for the feet.

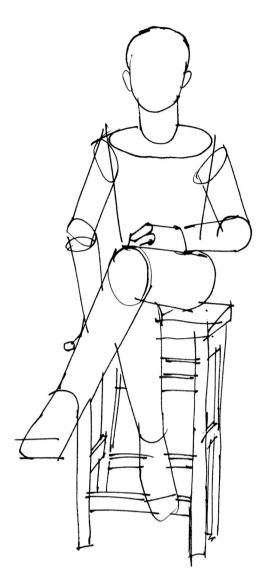

The "Tin Man" method works especially well when you are drawing people in complicated poses. It helps you to see the positions of the limbs more clearly.

Using the simple drawing as a guide, you can now start to draw your model's clothes. The artist has done this in the picture on the right.

When the drawing is finished, rub out the guidelines.

Now try drawing some "Tin Men" of your own in lots of different poses.

People moving

Drawing people who are moving may seem difficult at first. But it's like learning to ride a bike – the more you practice, the easier it becomes. And moving figures can make your pictures really exciting!

Before starting to draw a moving figure, spend some time just sitting and watching. Concentrate all your attention on the action of the figure, and how the legs, arms, head, and back are positioned. Notice how the balance of the body changes during the action. Perform the action yourself if it helps. Now try a lot of quick sketches. Don't worry about mistakes – the important thing is to catch the shape and expression of the body.

Nikki, aged 8, made this chalk drawing of a runner. He looks as if he is going to sprint right off the page!

When you draw figures in action, try drawing sweeping lines that follow the direction of the motion. This will help you to convey a feeling of speed and movement, and make your figures seem more realistic.

Hands up!

Hands are bigger than you might think. Look in a mirror and hold your hand up in front of your face, with your wrist resting on your chin. You will see that, from the wrist to the fingertips, your hand is almost as long as your face and about half as wide.

Hands seem difficult to draw at first because they are a funny shape. Three main shapes make up the hand. They are the thumb, the fingers and the palm area. Begin by drawing these sections as simple shapes, as shown on the right. Once you have drawn these shapes, you can start to add more details and shading to make them look more realistic.

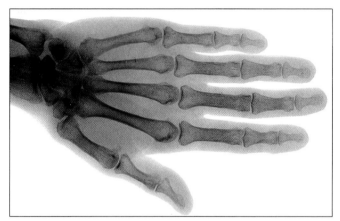

This X-ray picture shows the bone structure of the hand. The finger bones fan out from the wrist.

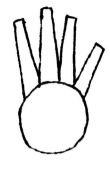

1 Start with a circle for the palm.

2 Add on the fingers (notice that the middle finger is the longest).

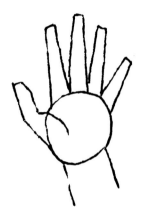

3 Add on the thumb. It is much shorter than the other fingers.

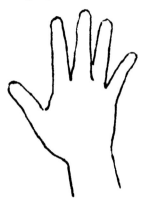

4 Now draw the hand and finger shapes properly and rub out your pencil guidelines.

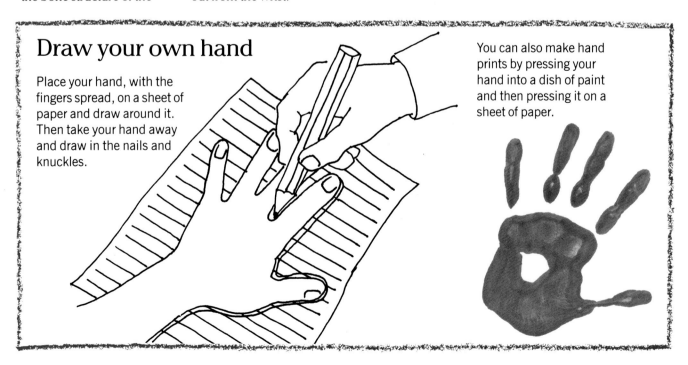

Draw your own hand

Place your hand, with the fingers spread, on a sheet of paper and draw around it. Then take your hand away and draw in the nails and knuckles.

You can also make hand prints by pressing your hand into a dish of paint and then pressing it on a sheet of paper.

Feet First

We don't take much notice of our feet, probably because they are usually hidden inside shoes and socks. But when you draw and paint people, it is important to know how to draw both bare feet and feet wearing shoes.

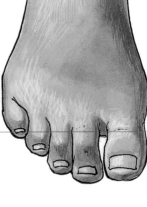

Make drawings of your friends' feet, from different angles. Try to fill the whole page with one drawing.

A foot seen from the side

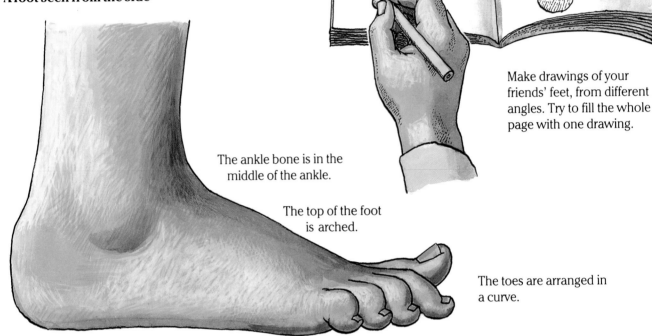

The ankle bone is in the middle of the ankle.

The top of the foot is arched.

The toes are arranged in a curve.

A foot seen from the front

The inside ankle bone is higher than the outside ankle bone.

The foot looks shorter than it does when we see it from the side.

The big toe has only one joint. The others have two.

This X-ray picture of a foot shows how many small bones it contains.

The ends of the toes have rounded pads.

Shoes come in all shapes and sizes. Here are just a few. How many other kinds can you think of?

Foot prints

If you look at the soles of boots and sports shoes, you will see that they have interesting raised patterns, called treads. You can use these patterns to make foot prints.

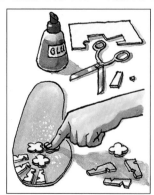

Get a friend to wear a pair of boots or sports shoes and stand on a sheet of cardboard or stiff paper. Draw around the edge of the shoes; then cut out the shapes.

Using scraps of things such as corrugated cardboard, string, cork, or plastic foam, copy the shapes of the raised patterns on the soles. Then glue them onto the sole shapes.

Brush the raised patterns with poster paint and make prints on paper. See how many different patterns you can collect.

Drawing yourself

If you want to learn more about drawing portraits, a good way is to set up a mirror and draw yourself. As you don't have to ask someone else to pose for you, you can work on your drawing any time you like.

A dresser mirror is useful because you can rest your drawing board on the edge of the table and the mirror is just the right distance away from you. Settle yourself comfortably and make sure there is plenty of light to work in.

Try out different poses. Do you want to face the mirror, or sit slightly to one side? Do you want to include only your face, or your neck and shoulders as well?

Before you begin your portrait, look closely at your face in the mirror and make sketches of your features. What shape are your eyes? How far apart are they? Is your mouth big or small? Try out different expressions. As you change expression, watch how your eyes, eyebrows, cheeks and mouth move and change shape. By getting to know your face in this way, you will find it easier to draw a good likeness.

Rest your drawing board at an angle so you don't have to move your head too much when you look up from your drawing to the mirror.

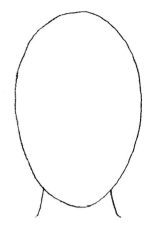

1 Start by drawing an egg shape for the face, and add the neck. Draw very lightly because you might want to make corrections later.

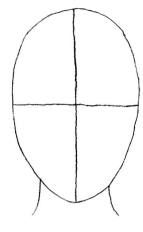

2 Draw a line down the middle of the head. This will help you to position the nose. Draw another line across the middle for the eyes to rest on.

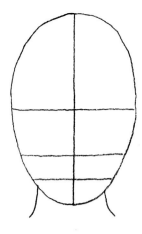

3 Draw a line halfway between the eye line and the chin where the tip of the nose will come. Draw another line between the nose line and the chin. This is where the mouth should go.

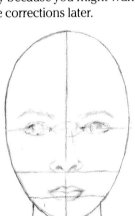

4 Draw rough shapes for the eyes, nose and mouth. Check that they are the right size and in the correct position. On most people, the eyes are about one eye-width apart.

5 Now you can start to fill in the details and draw the hair. Look for the areas of light and shadow. First shade in the light areas with light pencil lines.

6 Finally shade in the darkest areas. Don't forget to give your portrait a background.

Mixing color

When you decide to paint something, you must look carefully at the subject and try to see all the different colors and shades within it. Then you have to know how to mix the colors you see in it using the paints you have. It is important to learn how paints mix, because it will help make your paintings more realistic. It also saves you money, because from just a few tubes of paint, you can make many different shades and tones, simply by mixing different colors together. These pages will show you how to mix paints to get all the colors you need.

A rainbow is made up of seven colors: red, orange, yellow, green, blue, indigo (dark blue), and violet (purple), in that order. All the colors you see around you are made from these colors.

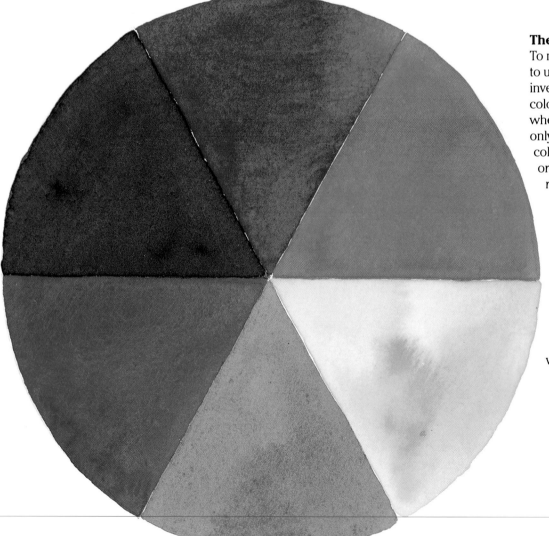

The color wheel
To make color mixing easy to understand, artists invented an idea called the color wheel. The color wheel is like a rainbow, only made into a circle. The colors are in the same order as they appear in a rainbow. You can make your own color wheel using watercolors (poster paints don't work very well for color mixing). Draw a circle, and divide it into six equal sections. Color the sections red, orange, yellow, green, blue, and violet (purple).

Looking at your color wheel, you will make some interesting discoveries about color mixing.

violet is mixed from red and blue.

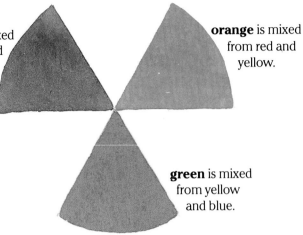

orange is mixed from red and yellow.

green is mixed from yellow and blue.

Primary colors Red, yellow, and blue cannot be mixed from other colors. They are called *primary colors.*

Secondary colors These colors are made by mixing any two primary colors together.

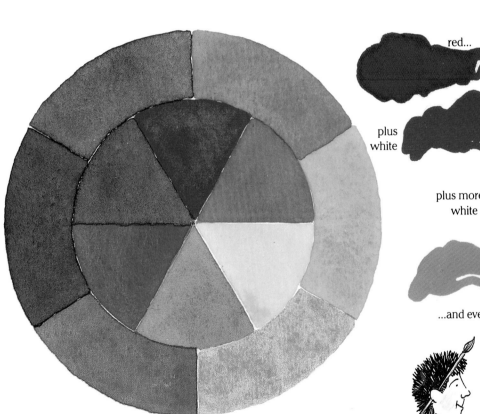

red...

plus white

plus more white

...and even more white

black has been added here

So, starting with the three primary colors – red, yellow, and blue – it is possible to mix lots and lots of different colors. Clever, isn't it! And you can make different shades of each color by adding a little black to darken them, or white to lighten them.

Mixing colors You can increase the colors on your color wheel to twelve, by mixing together any two colors that lie next to each other on the six-color wheel. This gives you what are called *tertiary colors* (pronounced "ter-shary"), which are red-orange, yellow-orange, yellow-green, blue-green, blue-violet, and red-violet.

Arty says...
Why not make your own color card like the ones paint manufacturers produce? Draw small squares on a sheet of paper, and fill them in with all the exciting colors you have mixed. Give each color an appropriate and descriptive name, such as "rebellion red," or "soggy cabbage green."

23

Painting skin

What color is skin? We might say that skin is "brown" or "white" or "pink" or "black." But when we look closely, we can see all sorts of colors in our skin – including gray, green, and blue! This is because skin reflects the colors around it. Test this for yourself by looking at the back of your hand in bright sunlight and then in shadow – see how the color of your skin appears to change? Look especially at the shadowy parts – do they sometimes look bluish or greenish? Next time you paint people, think about how you can mix your colors to make the skin look more realistic. These pages give you some tips.

Arty says...
Mix some paint, and see if you can match it to your own skin color. Test your mixture by dabbing some paint onto the back of your hand to see how closely it matches. Below are some blobs of paint of different skin colors.

Look for the light and dark parts of the skin – the highlights and shadows – and mix light and dark colors for each. This is how artists make their figures look real, as if we could reach out and touch them. Usually the parts that stick out, like the nose and forehead, are lighter, and the parts that go in, like the hollow under the bottom lip, are darker.

1 For this portrait, the artist first of all filled in the main areas of shadow, using blocks of dark color. The picture has been painted on colored paper, rather than white, which gives an interesting effect.
2 Next, some details were painted in and more highlights added with white paint.

3 On the finished picture, the shadows have been blended and the edges softened. Parts of the paper have been left to show through on some of the lighter parts of the face.

Right and wrong

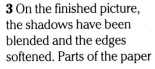 If you add black to make skin darker in the shadow parts, the color looks muddy and dead.

Instead, try adding a small touch of brown, blue, or green to the basic skin color for the shadow parts. You'll find it looks more realistic.

Skin color

Some people have very light skin, some have very dark skin, and others are somewhere in between. Here are three portraits of people from different ethnic backgrounds – see how the artist has used different color mixtures to paint each one.

Mixtures of brown, gray, blue and violet were used for this portrait. Black was used for the hair – but not for the skin.

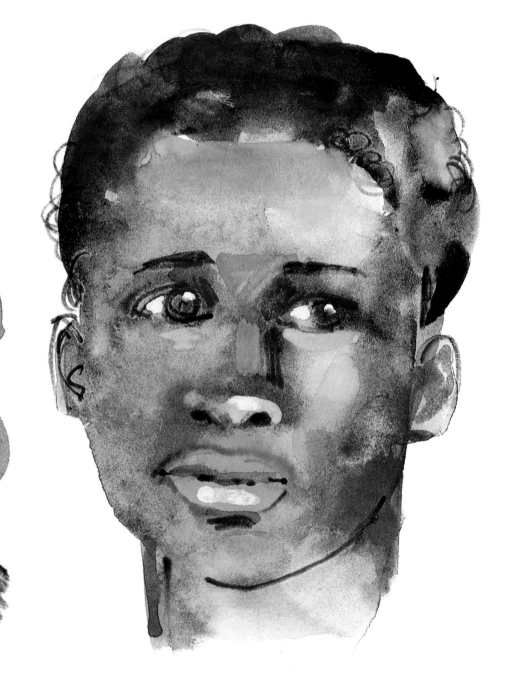

This girl has pale skin. The artist used yellow, pink and brown, and left some areas white, to model the shape of her face.

This man might be Asian or Latin American. His skin is a dark, warm brown. Notice how the artist has modeled the face with patches of dark brown, orange- brown and pinkish-brown. There are touches of green and blue, too, where the shiny parts of the skin reflect the colors around it.

Hair

When you are drawing hair, it is not a good idea to try to draw separate strands. This makes your subjects look as if they have spaghetti sprouting out of their heads! For a better effect, start by drawing the outline shape of the hair, then make a few lines and strokes in the same direction as the hair grows. Short curls can be drawn with groups of C-shaped strokes. Draw wavy hair with S-shaped strokes.

Notice the areas of light and shade on the hair (squint at them to see them better). The top of the hair is usually lighter, because light shines on it from above. The hair on one side of the head may be lighter if it faces the direction of the light.

If you are painting shiny hair, try leaving small areas of the white paper unpainted to show the highlights (see the girl in the blue sweater at the bottom of the next page).

Always use light, feathery strokes with your pencil or brush. If you press too hard, the hair will look solid and hard instead of soft.

Hair comes in many different styles – long and short, straight and curly, wavy and spiky. People's hairstyles help us to identify who they are. Men sometimes have beards, moustaches and bushy eyebrows, too. Here are some examples of different hairstyles – see how many you can spot next time you are out and about.

These pictures show step-by-step how to paint hair seen from the front and from the side.

Paint the head first. Make sure you get the proportions right. Then paint the outline of the hair.

There are several different methods you can use to express the texture of hair. Some of them are shown below.

Let the paint dry. Finally, add a few thin strokes with the tip of your brush.

While the paint is still damp, scratch into it with the end of your brush to indicate a few strands here and there.

Wipe most of the paint off your brush; then skim the brush lightly over the paper. This makes feathery, broken strokes that look like strands of hair.

Apply a thin wash of color. When it is dry, make light strokes over it with colored pencils.

Strokes of pastel or charcoal can be softly blended together with your finger.

With watercolor, you can paint one wash of color over another while the first is still damp. The colors mix together to create a soft effect.

Apply strokes of wax crayon and then scratch out some lines with a sharp point to indicate a few strands.

Spitting images

When you draw or paint someone's portrait, your aim is to make your picture look as much like that person as possible. If you do a portrait of your friend Tim, and your other friends say "Wow, that's the spitting image of Tim!" you can feel very proud of yourself, because getting a good likeness of someone is not easy!

So what is the secret? Before you begin drawing, take a good long look at your model. What do you notice first about him or her? Is it the hair, the eyes or the mouth? How long is the hair, and exactly what color is it? Is the face long and thin, or is it round? Are the eyes large or small? What shape is the nose? Is the mouth wide, or small and button-like? Does your model have freckles? These are the kinds of questions you should ask yourself; look at each individual feature carefully before you draw it.

You might like to start by drawing the shape of the face first. Or you might prefer to draw the eyes, nose and mouth and then draw the face around it. Keep looking back at your model while you draw, and keep checking all the time that you have got the shapes right and the features in the correct position.

Below are paintings of six different children. What are the most noticeable features of each one? (Answers below each picture.)

Blond curly hair, dark eyes and freckles. Wearing a green turtleneck sweater.

Dark hair, blue eyes and a red nose. Wearing a red scarf, tied cowboy-style.

Black curly hair and freckled red cheeks. Wearing blue-rimmed glasses and a shirt and tie.